NEW ZEALAND
FISH OF THE WEEK
NGĀ IKA O TE WIKI

GILLIAN & DARRYL TORCKLER

Monday's fish glides over the weed.

WHAI KEO/EAGLE RAY — These flat fish move their triangle-shaped wings up and down like a bird flapping its wings to swim through the water.

Tuesday's fish swims past at great speed.

TAKEKETONGA/ STRIPED MARLIN — One of the fastest fish in the sea, they swim north to warmer waters each winter.

Wednesday's fish holds on very tight.

MANAIA/SEAHORSE — Male seahorses carry baby seahorses in their abdomen until they are ready to be born.

Thursday's fish has a powerful bite.

MAKO/MAKO SHARK — The fastest shark in the ocean that must keep swimming to keep water flowing through its gills or it will die.

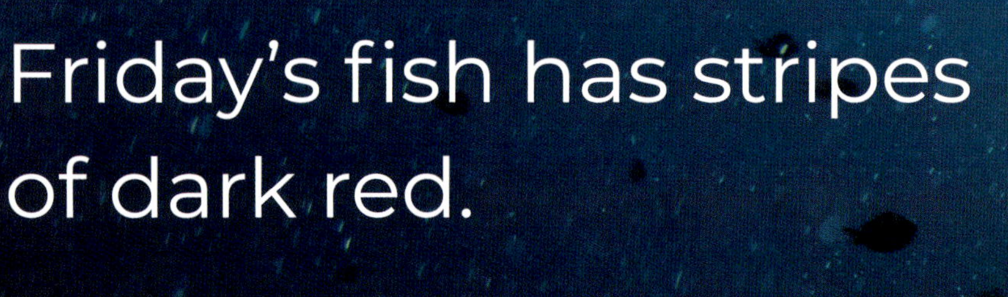

Friday's fish has stripes of dark red.

NANUA/RED MOKI — After finding a mate they live together along the rocky coastline for life.

Saturday's fish rests on the seabed.

RĀWARU/BLUE COD — Not related to other cod, the blue cod is indigenous to Aotearoa and very common along the South Island's coast.

But on Sunday, as the sun
shines bright,
aihe frolic together . . .

AIHE/COMMON DOLPHIN — Not a fish, but an air-breathing marine mammal that lives in all of the world's oceans.

. . . tāmure roam together . . .

TĀMURE/SNAPPER — The most popular of our food fish, even Captain Cook's crew reported catching and eating snapper in 1769.

. . . mātā gather together . . .

MĀTĀ/PINK MAOMAO — Swimming in dense schools they eat plankton during the day and rest on the rocky reef at night.

RĀTAPU | SUNDAY

. . . araara feed together . . .

ARAARA/TREVALLY — These silvery fish feed in closely packed schools and often create a disturbance on the water surface.

. . . petipeti float together . . .

PETIPETI/COMB JELLY — Not a true jellyfish, this harmless comb jelly has none of the stinging tentacles that true jellyfish have.

RĀTAPU | SUNDAY
. . . aua swim together . . .

AUA/YELLOW-EYE MULLET — Schools of mullet swim through estuaries and collect food from the sea floor as they go.

. . . haku hunt together . . .

HAKU/YELLOWTAIL KINGFISH — Growing as big as a human, these fish are expert hunters and chase school fish.

. . . maomao hover together . . .

MAOMAO/BLUE MAOMAO — Bright blue fish that gather in schools as they feed on plankton and rest out of the sun.

. . . while kōura rest.

KŌURA/SALT-WATER CRAYFISH — Salt-water crayfish are not fish but are crustaceans that shed (moult) their outer shell as they grow.

Published in 2025 by David Bateman Ltd
Unit 2/5 Workspace Drive, Hobsonville, Auckland 0618, New Zealand
www.batemanbooks.co.nz

ISBN 978-1-77689-137-5

A catalogue record for this book is available from the National Library of New Zealand.

Book design: David Bateman Ltd
Printed in China by Toppan Leefung Printing Ltd